More of
the World's
Best Golf
Jokes

More of the World's Best Golf Jokes

Ernest Forbes

Illustrated by Graham Morris

HarperCollins*Publishers*

HarperCollins*Publishers*
77–85 Fulham Palace Road,
Hammersmith, London W6 8JB

This paperback edition 1993
1 3 5 7 9 8 6 4 2

First published in Great Britain by
Fontana 1993

Text copyright © Ernest Forbes 1993
Illustrations copyright © Graham Morris 1993

The Author asserts the moral right to
be identified as the author of this work

A catalogue record for this book is
available from the British Library

ISBN 0 00 637934 6

Set in Goudy

Printed in Great Britain by
HarperCollinsManufacturing Glasgow

All rights reserved. No part of this publication may be
reproduced, stored in a retrieval system, or transmitted,
in any form or by any means, electronic, mechanical,
photocopying, recording or otherwise, without the prior
permission of the publishers.

This book is sold subject to the condition that it shall not,
by way of trade or otherwise, be lent, re-sold, hired out or
otherwise circulated without the publisher's prior consent
in any form of binding or cover other than that in which it
is published and without a similar condition including this
condition being imposed on the subsequent purchaser.

Acknowledgements

When starting this book it appeared to be a good idea to invite famous golfers to relate their favourite golf joke, so requests, stamped addressed envelopes and international postal coupons were speedily dispatched.

In view of the replies I received I wish to thank those golfers who did not reply and to the two who did reply; to the first, I would say what you suggest is a physical impossibility; to the second, I have no intention of placing my putter in such an unusable position.

A beginner was playing a short hole and was having a practice swing when his caddie tried to offer some advice. 'This is a short hole so perhaps . . .'

'Don't worry,' said the golfer sharply. 'I know what to do.'

The caddie remained quiet as the golfer struck the ball with great force and it whizzed through the air, struck a tree, ricocheted to a rock and then skimmed along the green to stop about four inches from the hole.

'Dammit,' snorted the golfer. 'I knew I should have hit it harder.'

The lady golfer slapped her male opponent across the face and shouted, 'When I asked you to give me a stroke a hole I meant in the golfing sense!'

Victor arrived early at the clubhouse to play his foursome and decided to have a drink. One drink led to another and by the time his companions arrived Victor was somewhat inebriated.

The game started and Victor was left with a long putt on the first green. As he prepared to putt, a large black shaggy dog ran on the green and stood between the ball and the hole. Victor took no notice of the dog and played his shot. The ball ran true, passed between the dog's legs and dropped into the hole.

'Wow!' cheered Victor's partner. 'That was a great shot, Victor, but why didn't you wait for the dog to clear off?'

'Christ!' exclaimed Victor. 'Do you mean to say that dog was REAL?'

The unpleasant visitor was studying the ball and the distance to the green.

'Well, caddie,' he asked for the first time, 'what do you think?'

'Well, sir, I advised the Prime Minister to use an eight from here yesterday,' answered the caddie.

The golfer took the eight and played his shot, which fell far short of the green.

'I thought you said you told the Prime Minister to use his eight here yesterday?' stormed the irate golfer.

'I did, but he didn't reach the green either.'

A doctor who was playing golf answered an appeal to go the locker room and there he found another member, George, lying on a bench, face down with a putter rammed up his backside.

'What the hell happened, George?' gasped the doctor.

'Well,' moaned George, 'I was playing golf with my girlfriend. It was her first time to play. I reached the green in three but her second shot landed about two inches from the cup. I bent over to pick up her ball and said, "It looks like your hole, darling," and that's all I remember.'

Harry Scott hooked his ball right across to the next fairway, almost hitting another golfer.

'Sorry about that,' yelled Scott, 'but I did shout "Fore". Why didn't you duck, I could have killed you?'

'Wouldn't have mattered,' came the sad reply. 'I took twelve at the last hole.'

Charles had to appear before the club committee on a charge of punching another club member.

'Charles,' said the chairman, 'this is a most unpleasant situation, to have to ask you to appear before this committee because you hit Robert Greer. This is the first time you've ever been involved in a matter like this. Perhaps you would care to explain.'

'Well,' replied Charles, 'it was the night of the Christmas party and if you remember it had been snowing and Robert went out and peed "Merry Christmas" in the snow.'

'But a lot of members did that,' pointed out the chairman.

'Yes, but his was in my wife's handwriting,' snorted Charles.

The telephone rang in the clubhouse and was answered by the bar steward. 'Castlekulm Golf Club.'

'Could you tell me if my husband is there?' a woman caller enquired.

'I'm sorry madam, you husband is not here,' replied the bar steward.

'How do you know, when I haven't told you his name?' protested the caller.

'Simple, madam,' said the bar steward, 'under a club rule a husband is never here when his wife telephones.'

Ginger Robinson sat at the clubhouse bar staring sadly at his drink.

'You look very depressed tonight, Mr Robinson, anything wrong?' asked the bar steward.

'You know John Simms who plays here?' said Ginger.

'Yes, indeed,' replied the steward. 'He plays a lot of golf with you.'

'That's right. Well he and my wife have run away together,' announced Ginger.

'You'll replace her,' said the steward, at a loss for words but trying to be comforting.

'Yes, I'll replace her but not him,' sobbed Ginger. 'You see, he was the only player in the club I could beat!'

The two golfers had imbibed rather freely before their game and made their way unsteadily to tee off. They had reached the fifth green when one player accused the other of cheating.

'Cheating,' slurred the other golfer, 'who's . . . cheating? I'm not cheating.'

'Then who's tilting the green?' charged the first golfer.

The accommodation committee had just started and the chairman stated, 'I'm sure the members will be pleased to note we have purchased a ball washing machine and hope to have it installed next week.'

'Surely,' protested one of the lady members, 'this is a blatant case of sex discrimination?'

Fields was in conversation with one of the leading golfers in America on the eve of a big tournament.

'If I win,' said the golfer, 'the prize money is good and I'm going to smother my wife in furs.'

'Wouldn't it be cheaper to use a pillow?' asked Fields.

Two Spanish golfers, Juan and Carlos, had played golf together for ten years until one day Juan accused Carlos of cheating. Carlos was so angry he went and bought a gun and returned to the clubhouse and shot Juan.

'What have you done?' cried the secretary in horror. 'What have you done?'

'I have made a hole in Juan,' shrugged Carlos.

William Claude Dunkenfield, better known as W. C. Fields, would at times grace the golf course and on one occasion he was asked by an opponent, 'Will you accept that my ball is dead?'

'A singular question, my good sir, but I cannot comment on that nugatory object although I've long had my doubts about you,' came the reply.

One day on the sixth Fields played a terrible shot, hooking the ball deep into the trees.

'That's the same shot as you played yesterday,' rebuked his caddie.

'Not at all, my withered little friend, not at all. Yesterday I played that stroke after drinking a bottle of gin, today I played it after drinking a bottle of vodka,' replied Fields.

'Frankly,' said W. C. Fields, 'I'd rather play a nine-hole course as it uses up less valuable drinking time.'

A well-known film director approached Fields after a game and invited him to have a drink in the clubhouse. When they were seated and sipping their drinks, the director leaned towards the comedian and asked, 'How long have I been playing golf with you?'

'About ten years,' answered Fields, caressing his glass.

'So you've seen me play quite a lot.'

'That I have, that I have.'

'Well, I know I can count on you for honest advice,' confided the director. 'I'll be playing Sam G. very soon and I must beat him, so tell me, how do I cut about six strokes off my game?'

Fields thought for a moment then gave his profound opinion. 'I suggest you stop playing at the seventeenth hole!'

The vicar stopped the golfer as he walked out of a sports shop.

'Good afternoon, Harold,' said the vicar in a reproachful voice. 'I haven't seen you at church recently.'

'If it comes to that,' replied Harold, 'I haven't seen you at the golf club recently.'

Dennis Taylor, the world famous snooker player, was playing in a golf Pro-Am. As he approached the second green he studied the lie, then took a stance which meant he was not facing the green.

Nick Faldo whispered to him, 'You're not facing the right way so you won't get the ball on the green.'

'Well,' said Dennis, 'I don't intend going straight for the cup. I'm going to drive at the oak tree, cushion off on to the green, touch the pin and drop into the hole!'

I know I'm not the world's best golfer but recently when I telephoned a club member and asked him if he wanted a game he replied, 'Sorry, we already have a threesome.'

Whack!!! The ball landed in a thicket in the trees in what was an unplayable position. The red-faced player stood shaking his fist at it, then lifted it and gently lobbed it to a better position.

'Found it,' shouted the player and as he did so became aware he was being watched. Turning sharply, he saw the observer was an escaped murderer whose photograph had been in the newspapers.

The two men stared at each other then the golfer quickly put his finger to his lips and whispered, 'I won't tell if you won't.'

The member was called to see the president and the secretary of the club. The president shook his head sadly as he spoke. 'I had no choice but to speak to you on a very serious matter and, quite frankly, if you haven't a satisfactory answer you will have to appear before the full committee.'

'What for?' asked Philip.

'Well,' said the president, tapping his fingers on the table, 'Mrs Armstrong has lodged a serious complaint against you. Earlier today it would appear that when she was on the ninth green your ball nearly hit her and you hadn't shouted a warning. When you arrived on the green you used bad language, told her she shouldn't be there and insisted on putting before her even though she was on the green before you. Is that true?'

'Quite true,' replied Philip calmly.

'Dear, dear,' muttered the president, 'have you anything else to say?'

'Yes, she was playing the wrong bloody way around the course!'

I t was a torrential downpour and the two road workmen braced themselves against the rain and cursed it. Through the high railings they could see four golfers plodding along without a care in the world.

'Funny thing,' said one of the workmen, 'I always thought these railings were to keep the nutcases out.'

'G ood morning,' said the man cheerily as he walked into the pro's shop. 'I would like some clubs.'

'Certainly, sir,' said the professional. 'Right- or left-handed?'

'I don't know,' replied the man. 'I haven't played yet. Better give me a set of each.'

N ow remember,' said the husband as he played for the first time with his wife, 'I don't like to talk when I'm playing.'

'You don't need to,' retorted his wife, 'just listen.'

W hen Paddy was invited to shoot a round of golf he arrived carrying his shotgun.

'There appear to be a lot of birds around today,' grunted the heavy-handed golfer.

'Probably following us for the worms, sir,' observed the caddie.

Tony was mad about golf and his ideal holiday was to go abroad and play on a different course each day. One year he had chosen California, which was a first-time visit to America for him.

His first day in Hollywood he met Julia and it was love at first sight, the two were immediately attracted to each other and even discussed getting married before Tony returned to England.

'I must warn you, Julia,' said Tony, 'that I'm a golfaholic. I play every day and often spend the weekends away playing. I just want to be honest with you before we get married.'

'As you're so honest with me, Tony, I'll be honest with you,' replied Julia. 'I'm a hooker.'

'No problem there,' responded Tony. 'Just concentrate on keeping your backswing smooth and your wrists straight.'

The girl had been taking golfing lessons for two months and one day she asked the club's professional if she should continue.

'Continue taking lessons?' queried the professional. 'Of course you should. Swinging that club is great exercise, tones up the muscles, strengthens the back, makes you breathe more deeply, encourages graceful movement and you can enjoy the beauty of nature. Besides, some day you might hit the ball.'

Gerry, a new golf enthusiast, walked into the pro's shop and examined the equipment with what he thought was an experienced eye.

He was approached by the old professional who asked, 'Can I get you anything?'

'Well, yes,' came the lofty reply. 'I want a pair of golf socks.'

'You mean a set of golf socks,' said the professional. 'Golf socks are sold in sets of three.'

'Oh, why is that?'

'You might get a hole in one,' came the dry reply.

The husband and wife were both golfers but made it a rule never to play together. However, in a charity match they were paired and rather than upset the programme decided to play.

It was a hard fought foursome but they won due to some excellent play by the husband.

The wife was delighted and asked her husband, 'Well, how do you like my game?'

'I suppose it's all right,' grunted the husband, 'but I'd still prefer golf.'

The golfer, glass in hand, staggered into the secretary's office. His breath would have stripped paint off the walls as well as being a considerable fire risk. Drunkenly he poked the secretary in the chest and slurred, 'Give me one good reason why I can't beat the captain of the club.'

'Certainly,' replied the secretary quietly. 'You are the captain of the club.'

The new male club member joined the three ladies to make up a foursome. After the introductions the first lady drove off playing a lovely shot right up the fairway.

'Oh,' said the man, 'lovely shot.'

'Not bad for a woman player with a wooden leg, eh?' asked the player.

'A wooden leg? I don't believe it,' said the man.

'Well, have a look,' replied the woman, unscrewing her wooden leg. The man watched her in surprise as she screwed her leg back on.

The second lady to tee off also played a good shot, her ball landing close to the first ball.

'That's another very good shot,' exclaimed the man.

'Not bad for a woman player with a wooden arm, eh?' queried the second player.

'A wooden arm! You couldn't play a shot like that with a wooden arm,' challenged the man.

'Just watch,' said the second woman as she rolled up her sleeve and proceeded to screw off her arm.

'Really hard to believe,' said the male golfer shaking his head.

The third woman played the best shot of all.

'Have you something wooden too?' asked the man.

'I have a wooden arse,' came the reply.

'That I find hard to believe,' said the man.

'Well, play your shot and I'll show you. You can screw it off if you like,' offered the lady.

The man played his shot and as the first two players walked along the fairway he and the wooden-arsed lady disappeared into the woods. They were soon missed by their companions who went into the woods and found them.

Sure enough, he was screwing the arse off her.

'Are you going to play golf again?'
   'You know, darling, I've a standing arrangement to play golf with Tony, Tom and Harry every Saturday morning.'
   'Well, you might forget your golf some Saturdays and give me a hand with the shopping, housework and children. I work all week too, you know,' said her husband as he started to wash the dishes.

A debate in the House of Commons is like a game of golf. They go around for hours and end up where they started.

The two countrymen arrived in Dublin from the wilds of Kerry and were dazzled by the hustle and bustle of O'Connell Street and Gresham Street. They stopped at a shop selling sporting equipment and looked at a large glass jar filled with tees which was in the window. Alongside the jar was a notice:

Guess The Number Of Tees In
The Jar And Win A Grand Prize

'Shure, Mick, I'd like to win a grand prize,' observed Paddy.
   'So would I, Paddy, but I don't know what the prize is. Faith, I don't even know what those things are in the jar. What are they?' said Mick.
   'Dunno,' replied Paddy. 'We'll ask the man in the shop.'
   The two men entered the shop and were met by an assistant.
   'Can I help you?' asked the salesman.
   'Yes, sor, those things in the glass jar in the window, what are they?' asked Paddy.

'Tees,' came the one-word reply.

'Tees?' echoed Paddy. 'What are they for?'

'Golfers put their balls on them,' said the assistant.

'My God!' exclaimed Paddy. 'These city folk think of everything.'

The golfer was having a terrible time. He hooked and sliced and spent most of his time hacking his way out of the rough. He became more and more irate and every stroke was cause for a swear word, and advice from his caddie was greeted with a snarl. So the caddie remained quiet and allowed himself a little smile.

'If you smirk again,' growled the golfer, 'I'll hit you with a club.'

'I doubt it,' chuckled the caddie. 'You wouldn't know which club to use!'

'I believe you got the results of my tests from the hospital,' said Tim, sitting down to face the doctor.

'I'm afraid so,' said the doctor.

'Bad, eh?'

'With a back like yours, your golfing days are over,' shrugged the doctor.

'That's terrible,' moaned Tim. 'You know how much I love golf. We enjoyed a lot of good games together.'

'We certainly did. But no more golf for you,' said the doctor in a philosophical manner.

'Is there anything I can do?' pleaded Tim.

'Yes, sell me your clubs,' replied the doctor.

Frank had been a footballer and when he retired he started to play golf. Every week he played a couple of games with his three friends. One day he had driven into the woods and when playing out his ball struck a tree and rebounded straight back at him. Instead of ducking, Frank tried to head the ball, which struck him on the temple, and he was dead when he hit the ground.

At the graveside his three friends were mourning his passing to the great course in the sky, and one remarked, 'Old Frank never had the best of luck. Even his burial isn't right.'

'What do you mean by that?' asked one of the other mourners.

'Well, look at his grave, it's on a slope and you remember how much Frank hated a downhill lie.'

Eric was worried about his golf. His play wasn't getting any better so he went to see the professional. 'You've seen me play, you know where I'm weak. What should I do?'

'Well, first you should relax,' advised the professional. 'Give it up for six months.'

'And then?' questioned Eric.

'Give it up altogether!'

The old vicar was having a wretched time, he was really out of form, and he reached his breaking point when he landed in the sand trap. As he emerged from the trap, seven strokes later and very red in the face, he bit out through clenched teeth to his companions, 'Would one of you laymen say a few appropriate words for me?'

'Ronald, may I have a word with you in private?' the club captain spoke in a low tone.

'Certainly,' said Ronald, and the two men walked to a corner where they settled with their drinks.

'What is it?' asked Ronald.

'This is a most unpleasant situation,' said the captain in an apologetic manner, 'but a number of members have reported to me that you cheat when you're playing.'

'That's right,' agreed Ronald in a cheerful voice, 'I do cheat.'

'You admit you cheat?' said the surprised captain.

'Of course I do.'

'But why do you cheat?'

'Simple,' pointed out Ronald. 'I play golf for my health and the lower my score the better I feel, so I cheat.'

A stranger joined a threesome on a public course and was invited to play.

'Yes, I'd like to,' replied the stranger.

'What do you play?'

'Seventy-five,' he responded.

When they reached the twelfth hole the stranger picked up his clubs and ball and said, 'So long, chaps. I've got my seventy-five.'

Mr and Mrs Russell were on holiday in the country and were playing on a rural course. Approaching the seventh, Mr Russell sliced a ball, which landed behind a hay-shed.

Looking at the hay-shed and the position of his ball, Mr Russell said, 'I'll pick it up and take the penalty.'

'Look,' said his wife, 'the shed is empty so if we open the front and back doors you could play right through.'

So they open the doors and Russell thumped the ball, which struck a post in the shed, bounced off and hit Mrs Russell on the head and she died on the spot.

About two years later Russell was playing the same course with a friend. Once again his ball landed at the hay-shed and he offered to pick it up and take the penalty.

'Hey,' said his friend, 'the shed's empty and I could open the doors . . .'

'No, thanks,' interrupted Russell. 'I had the same lie a couple of years ago and it cost me three strokes!'

The club pro was advising his new assistant on the procedure to be used if a customer wanted a new set of clubs. 'The old hands will know exactly what they want. Usually it's a matter of changing a set one club at a time but if they want a full set, sell it to them. However, if a beginner wants a set I normally suggest a short set of seven clubs. Just because they are allowed to carry fourteen they think they should have them, little do they know they'll use about five.'

Shortly after the talk a little woman entered the shop and said she wanted to purchase a new set of clubs.

'Have you been playing golf very long?' asked the assistant.

'No, I'm just starting,' replied the small woman.

'In that case I suggest you take the short set,' advised the helpful assistant.

'No, thank you, I'll have the regular size set,' said the little woman. 'Because if I don't like the game I'll give the clubs to my nephew and he's quite a tall boy.'

The new Irish tea lady brought the manager his morning tea. On his desk were two golf balls.

'What are those?' she asked, indicating the golf balls.

'Golf balls,' replied the manager.

A few days later the manager left two new golf balls on his desk and as soon as the tea lady arrived she spotted them.

'I see, sir, you've shot another golf,' she observed.

'When you travelled abroad did you visit the Holy Land?' enquired Mrs Barrington.

'I didn't but my husband did. He wouldn't return home until he had played St Andrews,' replied Mrs Dow.

Reading a golf manual is like reading a sex book. It looks all right on paper but when it comes to the real thing the strokes never go as smoothly as they should.

The golfer went to see his doctor, who was also a golfer, to find out the results of tests taken at the hospital.

'Good morning, Robert,' greeted the doctor. 'As I told you on the telephone, the results of your hospital tests have arrived.'

'The news must be bad when you wouldn't tell me on the telephone,' said Robert.

'Well,' acknowledged the doctor washing his hands, 'I've some bad news and some good news.'

'Let's hear the bad news,' suggested Robert.

'Owing to your accident, one of your testicles will have to be removed,' advised the doctor.

'And the good news?' enquired Robert.

'That should permit you to play off half-way between the men's and the women's tees,' commented the doctor cheerfully.

The golfer walked into the pro's shop and looked at some putters. Selecting a putter he asked the pro, 'Does this club have a guarantee?'

'Oh, yes, sir,' answered the professional. 'I guarantee it's a club.'

Major Smithers walked up to the secretary of the golf club and with a gentle nudge asked, 'Who is that new member?'

'Ah,' replied the secretary, 'he's the gravedigger who won two million pounds on the football pools.'

'Well, that answers it,' said the major. 'I wondered why he spat on his hands before playing a shot.'

'What goes putt, putt, putt?'
    'A bad golfer.'

The vicar greeted the man in a very friendly manner and said, 'Ah, Henry, I was delighted to see you in church last Sunday even if it was only to retrieve your golf ball.'

The two ragged old tramps sat on a park bench, each munching a stale sandwich.

'I used to live a life of luxury,' sighed one tramp. 'Then, as head of investments, I made the mistake of doing business with a foreign bank which went broke.'

'I also lived a life of luxury,' muttered the other old tramp, sadly shaking his head. 'Then I made the mistake of beating the boss at golf.'

My husband has left me,' sobbed Rita.
'Don't worry,' assured Brenda. 'He'll be back. He's been away before and always returned.'

'He won't return this time,' wept Rita. 'He's taken his golf clubs.'

Why', asked the firefighter, 'didn't you try and assist your wife when you saw her struggling to get out of the window to escape from the fire?'

'I couldn't,' replied the man. 'I was carrying my golf clubs at the time.'

You know,' said the boastful club bore to the stranger, 'I'm an excellent golfer. Last year I helped Ireland to beat Scotland.'

'Really?' drawled the stranger. 'Which team were you playing for?'

He strode out to the first tee with all his new gear and surveyed the scene. 'You know,' he said to his caddie as he squared up to the ball, 'as this is my first game it would really surprise my friends in the clubhouse if I got a hole in one with my very first stroke.'

'It certainly would,' observed the caddie, 'considering you're facing the wrong way!'

A golfer is a person who can express his thoughts to a tee.

'Quite frankly, old man,' said one golfer to his partner as they walked from the clubhouse, 'when you said you were going to give me your old bag I didn't think you meant your mistress.'

Bill hobbled painfully into the locker room and said to the three other golfers, 'I don't think I'll be able to play today, the old haemorrhoids are giving me bloody hell. Sorry if I have ruined your game.'

'Well, if it's instant relief and no pain you need to get you around the course, let's try the tea-leaf remedy,' suggested Mike.

'The tea-leaf remedy?' queried Bill. 'What's that?'

'Never heard of the tea-leaf remedy?' asked Mike. 'Tell him, Tom.'

'We pack the offending area with wet tea leaves, tape them in position and away you go. Only a temporary measure, you understand. You'll have to go and see your doctor as usual,'

explained Tom.

The operation was carried out and Bill was able to play the match with only slight discomfort.

When Bill went to the doctor the following day the medical man looked very pensive after the examination.

'Trouble, doctor?' asked Bill.

'The usual. I'll give you some ointment to apply,' said the doctor thoughtfully. 'As well as that, I can tell you that you will come into a large sum of money, you will cross water and meet a beautiful girl and your lucky colour is green.'

H arry shot a hole in one and it became his chief topic of conversation. After several weeks of listening to him tell how he did it, his wife was fed up with the story.

One night he was telling some visitors the tale and one of them exclaimed, 'That's wonderful. It must have been a great thrill.'

'Yes,' said Harry's wife tiredly. 'It's a pity he can't have it stuffed.'

G ive me my golf clubs, a good course, the fresh air and Michelle Pfeiffer as my partner, and you can keep my golf clubs, the good course and the fresh air.

D enis led his dog into the bar at the clubhouse when he was stopped by Harold, a member of the house committee.

'Denis, you know the rules. You're not allowed to bring a dog into the clubhouse,' warned the committee member.

'Ah, Harold, you'll want to hear this dog,' said Denis, 'so will the other members. This is Snead and he can talk, but not only can he talk he can answer questions on golf.'

'He'll have to go,' ordered Harold.

'Just one question,' urged Denis.

'All right. One question,' agreed Harold.

'And if he answers correctly you'll buy me a drink,' bargained Denis.

'All right. Get on with it.'

'Right,' said Denis addressing his dog, 'what's the opposite of smooth play?'

'R-rruff,' went the dog.

'See,' pointed out Denis. 'What about another drink for another question?'

'Yes,' nodded Harold, 'because that last question meant nothing.'

'What are you in when you use a seven iron?' asked Denis.

'R-rruff,' the dog went again.

'That's two drinks you owe me,' declared Denis.

'Nonsense, those weren't answers,' stated Harold. 'Double or quits if I ask the question.'

'Right, double or quits,' agreed Denis.

'You're on,' grinned Harold. 'Right now Snead, who is the best golfer playing today?'

'R-rr,' started the dog, then continued, 'many people would say that Severiano Ballesteros is the best but frankly I favour Nick Faldo.'

The young golfer stared vacantly at his locker. His older partner, trying to put his sock on in such a manner that his big toe wouldn't stick out, asked, 'What's bothering you? I hope you're in good nick as the pair we're playing are in great form.'

The younger golfer shut his locker door. 'I'm getting married shortly,' he replied.

'Oh, hell!' grunted the older golfer. 'That's enough to knock anyone off form. Well, welcome to the club. Having doubts?'

'I don't know if she's a virgin.'

'You don't know if she's a virgin?' exclaimed the surprised golfer.

'No, I don't,' confirmed the young man.

'Does it matter?'

'To me it does, and I can't very well ask her, can I?'

'No, I don't suppose you can, but if it's all that important to you go round to the pro's shop and tell Jack to give you a virgin kit,' said the older golfer, giving up the task of trying to hide his big toe.

'I never heard of a virgin kit,' admitted the young golfer.

'Well, Jack will fix you up.'

The pro's shop was empty as the young golfer entered and asked, 'Jack, can you give me a virgin kit?'

'Sure,' said Jack, handing over a box.

The young golfer opened the box to find a centre-shaft putter and two small tins of paint, one red and the other green. 'What am I supposed to do with this lot?'

'Well,' said the professional, 'on your wedding night, paint one of your testicles red and the other green and if your bride says, "I never saw balls like that before," hit her with the putter.'

The girl who arrived for golfing lessons was an exceptionally well-built young lady and had an enormous bust to prove it.

The professional watched her as she tried to swing at the ball. Her first attempt was a disaster, as was her second swing.

'Just one moment, miss,' said the kindly professional. 'You will have to decide whether you're going to play over or under them.'

The woman had retired from politics and decided to take up golf and accompany her husband, who was a golf fanatic. Her husband was giving her advice on putting and adjusting her stance, as much as she would permit him, then he said, 'Now, Margaret, think carefully of the line, then putt, think of the line, then putt, think putt, think putt, think putt.'

'What?' exploded his wife. 'You want me to think and putt at the same time?'

Johnny had just hacked his way out of a sand trap and his ball was lying about twenty feet from the hole. 'Traps are bloody annoying, aren't they?' he commented.

'They sure are,' replied Tom, lining up a two-foot putt. 'How about shutting yours?'

Mrs Hopkins had lost her ball and shouted at her caddie, 'Why didn't you watch where it went, you stupid little boy?'

'Frankly, missus,' replied the caddie, 'it usually doesn't go anywhere so it took me by surprise.'

'I lost a brand new ball this morning,' moaned the Scotsman. 'Oh? What happened? Knocked it into the rough?' enquired the Englishman.

'Nay, the string broke.'

The golfer was playing a shot about two feet from the edge of the water. Suddenly he slipped and fell in. As he sat and cursed in the water his opponent asked, 'How did you come to fall in?'

'I didn't come to fall in,' yelled the soaking player. 'I came to play golf.'

The man stopped at the church as the coffin was carried out. The coffin was placed in the hearse and flowers positioned around it. On top of the coffin a set of clubs was placed.

The man tapped a mourner on the shoulder and asked, 'Was the deceased a famous golfer? He must have loved the game when they're going to bury his clubs with him.'

'He still loves the game,' the mourner replied. 'That's his wife being buried. Those are his clubs. He tees off immediately after the funeral.'

It was a beautiful Sunday morning and Paul and John were enjoying their game of golf. However, on the twelfth green Paul admitted to a feeling of guilt that he was playing golf and didn't go to church.

'I couldn't have gone to church this morning, anyway,' said John. 'My wife is very sick.'

As the golfer sank his ball on the eighteenth green he threw his putter down in disgust and moaned, 'Such a day. I have never played so badly. I'll never be able to hold my head up again.'

'Oh, I don't know, sir,' said the caddie. 'You've been doing it all afternoon.'

It was a laughing matter at the club. The little idiosyncrasy of the professional was that when he was giving golfing lessons, every so often he would take off his cap, stare at the lining, replace his cap and continue teaching. It was generally accepted this was a superstition he had until one day his cap blew off and was picked up by a member. The member looked inside the cap to see a piece of paper taped to the lining; on the paper were the words – 'A hook shot goes left, a slice goes right.'

Dick and Arthur approached the first tee for their long-awaited game. Both men were good players, each determined to win, and betting was heavy in the clubhouse.

Dick was fully aware of Arthur's little ploy of breaking wind just as his opponent was about to play a shot, particularly a match-winning shot.

They reached the eighteenth hole and Arthur had lived up to his nickname of Windcheater during the play.

At the eighteenth Dick had to sink a two-foot putt to win. He examined the line, looked at the grass, rubbed his putter, took his stance, moved his feet, rubbed his putter again and eventually played the ball. It trickled down to stop about two inches from the hole.

'Bloody hell!' yelled Dick at Arthur. 'That's your fault, you and your farting!'

'But I didn't fart,' protested Arthur.

'No, but I allowed for it,' complained Dick.

The golfer had a horrendous round and as he walked to the clubhouse pondered on whether to give up golf and take up fishing, or take the easy way out and commit suicide.

'May I have your autograph?' The golfer's thoughts were interrupted by a man offering a pen and paper.

'You want my autograph?' asked the surprised golfer.

'Yes,' replied the man, 'so that whenever I play a bad round I'll look at your signature and know there's somebody who once felt worse than I do.'

'Pity Charlie didn't turn up,' said Reg, 'means we can't play a foursome.'

As he spoke, a little old man, bent of shoulders and slow of step, emerged from the clubhouse.

'I believe you're a player short, would you mind if I joined you?' asked the little man.

For a moment there was an uncomfortable silence then James spoke. 'You can be my partner.'

And so the match started and to the great delight of James the little old man had a powerful drive, his fairway shots were excellent and his putting was a treat to watch.

'You're a wonderful player,' praised James. 'You must have played a lot.'

'Not really,' replied the man, 'but anything I do I give it my

all. Life is for living.'

'Indeed,' agreed James. 'Sad to say most people don't realize that.'

'Well,' said the hunched little man, 'when I was twenty I was involved in an accident and I nearly died and from that day I've lived the full twenty-four hours. I smoke a hundred cigarettes a day, drink at least three bottles of gin a day and go to bed with five or six women every night.'

'What a life you've led,' exclaimed James. 'What age are you?'

'Twenty-four.'

The telephone rang in the solicitors' office and the receptionist answered, 'Allen, Tate and Porter.'

'Good morning,' the caller said. 'Is Mr Tate there?'

'Who is calling?' the receptionist asked.

'This is Gower, France and Hall. Mr Gower calling.'

'Just one moment and I'll connect you,' said the receptionist.

'Hello, Mr Tate's office,' his secretary said.

'Mr Gower is calling Mr Tate,' the caller said. 'Will you put Mr Tate on please.'

'Mr Tate is here,' his secretary said. 'Will you put Mr Gower on please?'

'Mr Gower?' the voice queried. 'Ready with Mr Tate.'

'Hello, Dave, this is Tim,' Gower said. 'Just checking that you haven't forgotten we tee off at two today.'

'Didn't forget. See you there. Bye.'

Mrs Barr was pulling out the lawnmower to do some gardening when her husband walked out and gently placed his golf clubs in the car.

'Golf! Golf! Golf!' shouted Mrs Barr. 'That's all you think about. While I'm mowing the lawn you're hitting a stupid little ball around the course. But I'm telling you, you'll play golf once too often and when you return I'll be gone – for good!'

'Now, now, dear,' replied Mr Barr softly. 'You shouldn't talk like that. You know very well you can't bribe me with promises.'

A golf club is a stick with a hard head at each end.

Ken Baker on holiday in Ireland was on the driving range with a bucket of balls and as he drove ball after ball he became aware someone was watching him. Turning, he saw a tall, well-built girl who looked like a female weight-lifter.

'Good-morning,' said Ken, raising his cap. 'Would you care to try a couple of shots?'

The girl accepted the club, took up an easy stance and swung at the ball. The ball sailed through the air and travelled about 330 yards, causing Ken to gasp in surprise.

'Would you like another shot?' asked Ken.

'Oh, yes,' answered the girl.

WHACK!

Again the ball soared through the air to cover about the same distance.

'That's a powerful drive,' said Ken shaking the girl's hand. 'My name is Ken.'

'Kitty,' replied the powerful girl as she cracked Ken's hand.

'Kitty, I'm arranging a mixed foursome for this afternoon, would you be my partner?'

'Oh, I can't play,' replied Kitty.

'I'll take that chance,' smiled Ken, thinking of the two powered drives.

After making arrangements with Kitty, Ken hurried off and collared Tom at the bar. 'About the mixed foursome this afternoon, is it still on?'

'It is if you have found a partner,' answered Tom. 'Two o'clock start.'

At two o'clock Tom started the match by hooking his ball into the trees and shouting, 'Bloody hell!'

'Right, Kitty, it's your shot,' chuckled Ken, placing the ball on the tee. 'Don't do what that silly bugger did and go into the trees, just hit the ball on to the green, near the flag will do.'

Kitty took her stance.

WHACK!

The ball climbed high and landed on the green about twenty feet beyond the hole.

'Great,' chortled Ken.

'Christ!' exclaimed Tom.

'Oh, my,' muttered Tom's partner.

When it came to putting time for Ken he was in a happy mood as he was in the lead. After carefully inspecting the line of play he played his shot and the ball ran past the hole by about a foot.

'Will we sink it?' Ken asked Tom.

'Why not?' shrugged Tom.

'Are you happy enough with this shot?' Ken asked Kitty as he handed her a putter.

'Sure, no bother,' said the girl taking her stance.
WHACK! . . . and the ball travelled another 330 yards!

It was the first time the golfer had played the course. He thought himself a much better player than he was and insisted on getting the best caddie.

As he played an unspectacular round he asked the caddie, 'Who was the best golfer to have played here?'

'Without a doubt, Ted Turner, sir,' replied the caddie without hesitation. 'He was never beaten.'

'Well, if I had a game with him today who do you think would win?' asked the boastful golfer.

'You would, sir.'

'You really think so?' beamed the golfer.

'Certainly do,' drawled the caddie. 'Ted Turner has been dead for two years.'

'How many were you at that hole?' asked Peter. 'Eight,' replied Paul. 'No, wait, I lie, it was seven.'

'Well,' retorted Peter, 'I'm putting you down as nine. There's a one stroke penalty for improving your lie.'

'I notice,' said James, leaning on the clubhouse bar, 'that each time you tell someone about your putt to win the competition last Saturday you change the distance.'

'Well,' said Ronnie, lifting his glass, 'I never tell a man more than I think he'll believe.'

'**I** got a birdie today,' announced the wife when she returned home from golf.

'Ah, one under par,' smiled her husband.

'No, I think it was a sparrow.'

A golfing friend is one who can remember every shot you missed but doesn't remind you.

As Graham was preparing to putt he was surprised to see a ball drop on to the green, bounce once and then slowly trickle into the cup.

A long-legged, long-haired blonde appeared and asked him if he had seen her ball.

'Yes,' answered Graham. 'It went right into the hole.'

'It did? Oh wonderful!' shouted the girl, waving her club madly. 'Little me got a hole in twenty!'

'**H**ello Joe,' greeted the golfer at the clubhouse. 'How's your game at present?'

'Christ, Richard, it's so bad that I'm going to hire a bucket of balls just to practise placing them on the tee,' replied the downhearted Joe.

Leslie got so mad when his ball landed in the pond that he threw his clubs and bag into the water and stormed off.

A few minutes later he returned, much to the pleasure of his friends.

'I knew you'd be back,' said one of his companions.

Leslie waded into the water and pulled at his bag, rummaged around, threw the bag back into the water and stalked away without speaking.

'What was all that about?' asked one of the players.

'I forgot my car keys,' shouted Leslie.

The golfer kissed his golf ball, placed it on the tee very gently and said to it, 'Let's try and make it this time Titanic.'

'Why do you call your ball Titanic?' asked one of the other players.

'You'll understand when we come to the water hazard,' said the first golfer.

Golf is a wonderful excuse for taking a walk and not having to take your wife or your children with you.

The manager of a sports equipment company approached a professional golfer and asked, 'For £50,000 would you endorse our golfing equipment?'

'For £50,000 I'd even use your equipment,' grinned the golfer.

He shot a hole in one and so, on reaching the clubhouse, he bought drinks for all the members and kept buying as more members arrived. Being a gentleman he always had a drink with them until suddenly he keeled over in a heap on the floor.

'He's drunk,' said one of the members.

'No, he's not,' said the golfer's partner. 'I saw his little finger move.'

One golfer I know plays in the afternoons during the week as he claims it's easier to get away from the office than from his wife.

George was a terrible golfer and had just returned from a month on safari in Africa. He walked into the professional's shop and said with considerable glee. 'I need some balls. Golly! I am really looking forward to this game. It'll be my first game for almost six weeks.'

'You'll hardly know the course now, George,' pointed out the professional. 'It's almost healed.'

The golfer was playing in his first club competition and was very nervous.

'Don't be nervous,' said the caddie. 'Just remember if your opponent was any good he wouldn't be playing you.'

The two Irishmen were on a motoring holiday when they decided to have a game of golf. They stopped at a small town and were directed to the council-owned golf course. After hiring clubs they prepared to tee off.

Shamus addressed the ball, swung strongly and shouted, 'Two!'

Mick looked at him in amazement and said, 'You're supposed to shout "Fore!"'

Shamus looked at Mick and said, 'Don't be daft! Shure isn't this only a nine-hole course!'

The visitor had just sat down when the clock struck five. He checked his watch and remarked, 'What's wrong with your clock? It's seven o'clock but it only struck five.'

'Nothing wrong with the clock,' replied the host. 'It's a golfers' clock. Automatically deducts two strokes.'

The police officer answered the telephone. 'Oldtown Police.'

'I want to report a robbery,' the caller stated.

'Yes, sir,' said the constable. 'May I have your name?'

'Sir Horace Pennington-Hall.'

'Ah, Sir Horace of Hall Manor?'

'That is correct.'

'What was stolen, Sir Horace?' questioned the constable.

'My favourite putter, a dozen new golf balls and my golfing cap which I have worn since my university days,' complained Sir Horace.

'When were they stolen, sir?' went on the police officer.

'This morning.'

'Where were they stolen from?'

'The boot of my car,' said Sir Horace.

'Am I right in saying you drive a Silver Mist Rolls Royce?' continued the constable.

'You are quite right.'

'So the thieves forced the boot of your car to steal your golfing equipment?' concluded the constable.

'No. They stole the car as well!'

The rather portly woman was learning to play golf and the professional was advising her on stance and swing. Then the professional placed a ball on a tee and invited the woman to hit it.

The woman swung and missed, swung and missed, swung and missed. Twelve times she missed.

'That's a dozen times I've swung at that ball and I haven't hit it yet,' panted the exasperated woman.

'Keep trying,' said the professional. 'I think a couple more swings and it'll go with the wind.'

Dave Mitchell had a terrible foursome, ending when he missed a six-inch putt. He stormed into the locker room, broke every club in his bag, threw his bag through the window, pulled out a hunting knife and slashed his throat.

Just then his companions entered the locker room and one asked, 'Want to play tomorrow, Dave?'

'What time?' Mitchell croaked, trying to stem the bleeding.

'Caddie, I suppose you've seen worse golfers in your thirty years at the club . . . caddie, I said I suppose you've seen worse golfers,' panted the struggling player.

'I heard you the first time, sir, I'm just trying to remember,' answered the caddie.

'Mrs Hunter said her husband had a moral victory playing golf yesterday,' said Mrs Powers. 'What does moral victory mean?'

'Finding a ball better than the one he lost,' replied her husband from behind the newspaper.

A letter to all members from the secretary of an Irish golf club:

In view of the increased fees for the forthcoming year the committee members feel that, to give you value for your money, it has been decided to make the holes smaller.

'That new chap, Minor, how's he doing?' the club captain asked the professional.

'Oh, he's a political golfer,' answered the professional.

'What do you mean – a political golfer?' enquired the captain.

'Promises a lot and does nothing.'

It was a Pro-Am match and one celebrity had played a terrible shot which had struck a tree and ricocheted into the branches of another tree, where it remained firmly lodged.

'How would you play that?' the celebrity asked his professional partner.

'Under an assumed name,' whispered his partner.

The golfer had been struggling all the way; it had not been a good day. As he approached the fourteenth he drove the ball deep into the woods.

'Dammit,' cried the golfer to the caddie. 'What do you suggest I use now?'

'How about an axe?' replied the caddie helpfully.

For weeks his wife had been nagging Norman about golf, away every weekend enjoying himself. It got to such a stage that he said he would take her to the course and teach her to play.

When the arranged day arrived the weather was terrible and by the time they reached the third green his wife was soaked, exhausted, completely fed up and wanted to go home.

'Now,' said Norman, 'perhaps you'll stop nagging me. You think I'm enjoying myself every weekend – now you can see what a hardship it is.'

'Carry your bag, sir?' asked the caddie.
'No, let her walk,' replied the husband.

'I find golf is very educational,' said the first wife.
'How is that?' asked the second wife.
'Well, every time my husband turns the television on to watch golf I go into another room and read a book,' replied the first wife.

'Jack doesn't love me at all,' cried the tearful wife.

'Now, now,' consoled her old school friend. 'I'm sure he loves you, why do you think he doesn't?'

'Well, we had a row about him playing so much golf and I said he would have to choose between me and his clubs.'

'And what happened?'

'He went to bed with his golf clubs!'

Jeff was in bad form when he came home.

'What's the matter dear?' asked his wife.

'Dr Hyde says I can't play golf,' growled her husband.

'Oh, dear,' gasped the anxious wife. 'Did he see you at the hospital?'

'No, playing golf.'

A player was preparing to putt when a ball whizzed past his ear and dropped on to the green. After the foursome had putted out, a woman golfer approached them and said to the golfer who had escaped injury, 'I'm sorry I didn't shout "Fore" as a warning but I didn't want to spoil your putt.'

Jack was hacking around in the rough for some time before the ball eventually clipped to the fairway.

'How many did it take you?' asked Robert.

'One,' replied Jack.

'But I counted twelve,' pointed out Robert.

'Not at all,' answered Jack with considerable aplomb. 'I took eleven to kill a snake.'

The woman as a golfer left a lot to be desired. She hacked, hooked, sliced and missed, but continued quite unaware that her caddie was nearing a nervous breakdown.

At last the eighteenth hole was reached and when the woman eventually putted the ball she said, 'I had a wonderful time. It was a most enlightening experience.'

'It certainly was enlightening,' replied her caddie. 'I've been a caddie here for twelve years and today I've seen places I didn't know existed.'

Major Grant and the vicar were having their weekly game and as usual the vicar was leading. The major noted that before each shot the vicar said a short prayer.

On the fourteenth green Major Grant had a long putt for par. He carefully studied the position then, preparing to putt asked, 'Vicar, would it do me any good to say a prayer?'

'I think not,' replied the vicar. 'I think not.'

'Why not?' snorted the major.

'Because you can't putt,' smiled the vicar.

It was a dreadful day on the course, a chilling wind with heavy rain beating against the players. As the husband and wife team struggled against the appalling weather conditions the wife gasped, 'Tell me again, Dick, what a wonderful time we're having. I keep forgetting.'

It was Ladies' Day and Maud was very excited, all she needed was to sink a two-foot putt and the Captain's Prize was in her possession. She examined practically every blade of grass between the ball and the hole. She fluttered her handkerchief to determine the exact direction of the wind, she polished her sunglasses, she balanced her putter and she wiped her hands. Finally she turned to her caddie and asked, 'How should I play this?'

'Keep it low,' grunted the caddie.

R ichard arrived at the club to find a new caddie waiting for him. The boy looked very young and inexperienced.

'Can you count correctly?' asked Richard.

'Yes, sir,' replied the caddie.

'Are you good at adding?'

'Very good at adding, sir,' said the caddie in a knowing tone.

'What's the total of 5 and 4 and 3?'

'Nine, sir.'

'Come along,' said Richard, 'I think we'll get along very well together.'

T he golfer arrived at the course and requested a caddie.
A young lad arrived to perform the duties and was asked by the golfer, 'Can you find lost balls?'

'Oh, yes, sir,' replied the caddie.

'Good. Then find one now and we'll make a start.'

T he pub was crowded and all the drinkers were watching the British Open on television.

'Turn up the sound,' someone requested.

'Sssh . . . ' said the landlord. 'Not while Faldo is putting.'

The husband parked his car and walked into the clubhouse to greet his wife after her first day at golf.

'Hello, darling,' said the husband. 'How did you do?'

'I shot seventy,' gurgled his wife.

'Seventy!' declared the husband in surprise. 'That is absolutely wonderful!'

'Yes, and tomorrow I play the second hole!'

The golfer completed his round in disgust and complained, 'That's dreadful! I've never played so badly before.'

'Oh,' said the caddie, 'you've played before then?'

She was a boorish, rude, overbearing woman, who, in the opinion of many of the club members, would be more suited to kick-boxing than golf. Her tee shots and putting were good but her fairway shots were atrocious so she went to see the professional at the club.

In her usual brusque manner she beckoned to the professional, indicating he should come over and speak to her.

'Good afternoon,' said the professional politely.

'I'm having trouble between my holes,' she barked.

'No use speaking to me about that,' replied the professional. 'Better go and see a doctor.'

It was August Bank Holiday and the day dawned bright, sunny and warm.

'It's a lovely day,' said Mrs Montgomery as she passed her husband his breakfast cup of tea. 'So perhaps we could go for a

drive to the sea. I didn't think you'd want to play golf today, after all you played yesterday and the day before. You weren't thinking of playing golf today, were you?'

'Golf? Golf?' answered her husband vacantly. 'Nothing could be further from my mind. Please pass the toast and putter.'

The man stormed into the professional's shop and threw a bag of clubs on the counter.

'Anything wrong, sir?' asked the professional.

'Anything wrong indeed! Just because I haven't played golf before, don't take me for a fool,' bellowed the man.

'I've no idea what you're talking about,' replied the puzzled professional.

'Don't come the old soldier with me,' shouted the man. 'You know what I'm talking about.'

'I really have no idea,' persisted the professional.

'You sold me this set of clubs this morning and they're all different,' yelled the man, thumping the golf bag.

As the two golfers approached the eighteenth hole one remarked, 'The flag is in a peculiar position.'

When they reached the green they saw the flag had been thrust into the chest of a man who lay moaning at the edge of the green.

'It's Tommy,' cried one player as they rushed to help.

'What happened, Tommy?' they both asked as they knelt beside the injured player.

'That Eric,' groaned Tommy, 'he's such a poor loser.'

Roger swung at the ball and sliced it. The ball struck a bird which immediately fell to the ground.

'Oh, dear,' gasped Roger. 'I've killed a bird.'

'Don't worry, sir,' said the caddie, 'it would have been killed by the fall anyway.'

'Well,' asked the husband as he polished his putter, 'how did the sermon go this morning?'

'Fine,' replied his wife. 'But tell me, does the vicar play golf?'

'Yes, he does,' said the husband. 'We belong to the same club. Why do you ask?'

'That's really what his sermon was about this morning. He used golf as an example of life and preached on the sinfulness of cheating at golf,' said the wife.

'Did he mention any names?' asked her husband anxiously.

The beginner was having a terrible round and worse was to follow when his ball lodged high in the branches of a tree.

'What will I take now?' asked the golfer, looking at his clubs.

'Frankly, sir, if I were you,' said the caddie, 'I'd take the next bus home.'

After much searching, the caddie found a ball in the rough and handed it to the golfer.

'This is not my ball,' declared the player. 'This is an old ball and mine was brand new.'

'Ah, yes, sir,' agreed the caddie, 'but don't forget it's a long time since we started out.'

'I'm resigning from the club,' declared the disgruntled member. 'The wife swapping parties being run in this club are an utter disgrace.'

'But you always joined in the parties,' pointed out the secretary. 'Indeed, if I recall correctly you are a founder member of this activity. So what happened to change your mind?'

'Well, you know the rule was to throw your putter in a heap, then you were blindfolded and you pulled out a putter and got the owner's wife,' went on the heated member.

'Yes,' agreed the secretary, 'that is correct. So what went wrong?'

'Some bastard stole my putter!' shouted the member.

Major Prentice was having trouble with his swing so he approached the professional with the problem and asked, 'How can I overcome my uneven swing which causes me to hook and slice?'

'You're bending your elbow too much,' said the professional.

'Are you telling me to keep my arm straight?' questioned the major.

'Yes,' answered the professional, 'particularly when you're at the bar.'

The ball had landed in a bunker and the golfer was determined to play out. He was hacking away madly and swearing loudly.

'Hey, Archie,' shouted his companion, 'are you trying to play out of that bunker or make an elephant trap?'

The two women were about to tee off when one remarked, 'Doris told me Andrew has given up golf. That really surprised me, I thought your husband loved golf.'

'He does,' answered the other woman, 'but he found it too stressful so he has taken up bungee-jumping instead.'

He was a powerfully built man who had not improved his game since he had taken up golf five years earlier. In this foursome the captain of the club was his partner and the big man prepared for his tee shot.

His swing was full and strong and the ball shot straight up. The four men watched it with undisguised interest as it stopped climbing and descended rapidly to land slightly ahead of them.

'You know, Tom,' declared the captain, 'in all my years playing golf, it's the first time I've seen a 300-yard drive rest four yards from the tee!'

The irate golfer turned to the caddie and snarled, 'I thought you said you were the best caddie in Middlesex.'

'I did, but the way you're playing I think we must be in Surrey by this time,' replied the caddie.

'How's your daughter's golf?' asked Mrs Green.

'Wonderful, thank you,' replied Mrs Brown. 'She's going round in less and less every week.'

'I don't doubt that,' smirked Mrs Green. 'But how's her golf?'

The vicar beckoned to the boy golfer who walked over to the railings.

'I wonder what your mother would say if she knew you were playing golf on Sunday?' rebuked the vicar.

'Why don't you ask her?' answered the boy. 'She's trying to play out of that bunker.'

I hate playing golf with Peter Temple. He can hit a ball farther than I go on holiday.

The beginner was doing his best but without success. He was lucky to move the ball at all.

'Excuse me,' said a friendly golfer, 'but you swing around too much. Let the club do the work.'

'Why tell me?' snapped the beginner. 'Tell the bloody club!'

Then there was the Irishman who loved golf and also believed in reincarnation. His dearest wish was that he would return to earth as a caddie.

He did – and now they keep tea in him.

The golfer had taken his young son to watch him play golf and on their return home the boy was asked by his mother if he had enjoyed watching his father play.

'Oh, it was great!' gushed the boy. 'And daddy got to hit the ball more than anyone else.'

'Be careful of those trees to the right of the fairway,' whispered Rosemary to her friend.

'Why?' asked Donna.

'That's where the caddies always try and slip away,' confided Rosemary.

The husband took his wife out for her first game of golf. Her stance was good, her swing perfect and the ball sailed gracefully through the air to land on the green and slowly trickle into the hole.

The husband followed with a par four.

The wife's second tee shot once again landed on the green and the ball ran up the slope, passing the hole, but on reaching the top of the slope it rolled gently back and dropped into the cup.

'Golly,' exclaimed the wife to her ashen-faced husband, 'I thought I had missed it that time!'

As they had done for the past twenty years, the four men set out for their Sunday game of golf. The rivalry was as keen as ever.

One golfer trying to hit out of a bunker suddenly collapsed and lay twitching on the ground.

'I say,' shouted another player, 'I think George is having a stroke!'

'Well, just make sure he marks it on his card,' said one of the other players.

'Ah,' said the vicar, 'tell me, Mrs Roberts, does your husband play a lot of golf?'

'Oh, I would say about seventy-two holes a week, roughly speaking,' answered Mrs Roberts.

'And how many would he play without using bad language?' enquired the vicar.

The two beginners were playing golf. The first man took a powerful swing and the ball sailed high in the air, fell on the green and with one bounce fell into the hole.

'That's a hole in one,' gasped his surprised partner.

'Yes, and I bet I can do it again,' said the boastful beginner.

'Right, that's a bet,' said his companion. 'But on one condition.'

'Sure,' agreed the player. 'What's the condition?'

'This time,' ordered his companion, 'you've got to play the shot with your eyes open!'

'My husband is very frank and outspoken,' said Molly. 'He calls a spade a spade.'

'So does mine,' nodded Ruth, 'but I couldn't repeat what he calls his golf clubs.'

Four golfers were playing on a course where the hazard on the fourteenth was a ravine. They drove off. Three of the golfers played into the ravine, the fourth got his ball over.

The three who had played into the ravine went to have a look and two of them immediately decided not to play their balls and forfeit the hole. The third golfer said he would go down and play out his ball. He disappeared down the ravine and presently his ball lobbed out, followed by the panting player.

'How many strokes?' asked one of his companions.

'Three,' gasped the breathless man.

'But we heard six,' said his companion.

'Ah, three of them were echoes!'

'In this case I think the three iron should be used,' suggested the caddie at a short hole.

'No, I'll use my driver,' said the golfer firmly.

'Should be the three.'

'Driver!'

The caddie handed over the driver and the golfer whacked the ball, which swerved to the left, struck a tree and bounced off to strike another golfer on the head after which it hit the green and sped along the surface to hit the pole and drop into the cup.

'See,' said the golfer. 'I told you the driver was the right club.'

'How did the play go today, Mrs Mills?' asked the professional.

'I missed the ball a few times,' confessed Mrs Mills, 'but that caddie didn't help. Every time I missed he would laugh. I felt like hitting him on the head with the club.'

'Perhaps you could,' said the professional thoughtfully. 'His head is certainly bigger than the ball.'

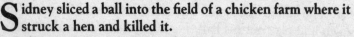

Sidney sliced a ball into the field of a chicken farm where it struck a hen and killed it.

Sidney was very upset and sought out the farmer. 'I'm sorry, my ball hit one of your hens and killed it. Can I replace the hen?'

'I don't rightly know,' replied the farmer as he rubbed his chin, 'how many eggs do you lay a day?'

'Oh, dear,' said the lady golfer after slicing the ball into the rough at the eighth. 'After all those lessons and I'm still not getting it right.'

'Have you been taking lessons?' asked her companion.

'I've taken twenty-five and it has cost me a fortune,' replied the first golfer.

'That's pretty rough,' observed her companion. 'You should see my brother-in-law.'

'Is he a golf professional?'

'No, a solicitor. Perhaps he could help you get your money back.'

'Goodbye,' said the dentist to his receptionist. 'I'm going to play golf so you can lock up early.'

Just then the telephone rang and the receptionist listened to the caller for a moment before replying, 'I'm sorry, the dentist couldn't possibly see you this afternoon, he's very busy, he has eighteen cavities to fill.'

BOING!

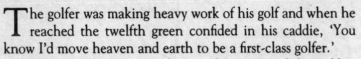

The golfer was making heavy work of his golf and when he reached the twelfth green confided in his caddie, 'You know I'd move heaven and earth to be a first-class golfer.'

'Well, you better start working on heaven,' said the caddie, 'because you certainly moved a hell of a lot of earth today.'

'You know,' said Mick, 'Paddy is so stupid that when he plays golf and has to address the ball he puts his postal code on it.'

'He's not all that stupid,' retorted Shamus. 'I can never remember mine.'

In the locker room the two golfers prepared to go out and do battle on the course and as John lifted his bag he said, 'Now just remember, Fred, that casual water means a temporary pool caused by rain, hail or snow; not going behind a tree for a pee.'

'You never saw such golf as that man played,' applauded Stewart. 'His drives were perfect, his approaches wonderful and his putting was out of this world. I would say he's one of the best golfers in the country.'

'Well, you don't mind being beaten by a player of that standard,' said Holt in a comforting tone.

'Beaten? Beaten? What are you talking about?' said Stewart. 'I wasn't beaten. I won.'

Alan greeted Edgar in the street. 'Hello, Edgar, I hear you have given up golf.'

'Yes, indeed,' agreed Edgar. 'Gave it up completely.'

'Golly! I wish I could give up golf, but it's got such a hold on me. How did you manage to give it up?' asked Alan.

'I went to a hypnotist and he took golf right out of my system and out of my mind. I never think of the game now,' stated Edgar.

'That's wonderful,' said Alan. 'I might try him. Where is his office?'

'Oh, a good drive and a short putt from here,' replied Edgar.

Clinton was a keen golfer but his wife did not share his enthusiasm and seldom missed the opportunity of reminding him of the time he spent at the golf club.

'You know,' she said in anger, 'if you were to spend a weekend, just one weekend with me, I'd probably die of shock.'

The husband grabbed his diary. 'Well, I'm playing in tournaments the next two weekends but what about the first weekend of next month?'

'My dad has dozens of trophies for golf,' said little Freddie. 'Is he a professional golfer?' asked his teacher.

'No, a pawnbroker,' replied Freddie.

One golfer spent so much time in the sand traps he was known to the other club members as Lawrence of Arabia.

'What did your husband say when you missed that short putt on the fifteenth?' enquired Winnie.

'Shall I leave out the swear words?' asked Betty.

'Yes.'

'Nothing,' sighed Betty.

Vice President Dan Quayle is an active golfer and when he plays he is guarded by secret service men who often adopt disguises.

During one match in which Mr Quayle was playing, his opponent remarked to him, 'You know, sir, in all my years of playing golf, that's the first time I've ever heard a tree fart!'

The man was about to swing at the ball when another golfer approached him and said, 'You can't drive off from there, that's the ladies' tee.'

'Shut up!' hissed the player. 'This is my second shot.'

Did you hear about the Irishman who took a lap of honour when he won his first major golf tournament?

Paulette was trying hard but obviously golf was not her game. She even had difficulty in remembering the names of the clubs.

Early one morning she and the pro started a game and she asked, 'When do I used my putter?'

'Sometime before dark, I hope,' came the weary reply.

Bob Hope claims he plays in the low seventies. If it's any hotter he stays indoors.

Mr Hope also observed, 'If you watch a game, it's fun. If you play it, it's recreation. If you work at it, it's golf.'

'Can I play now, dear?' the wife asked her husband.
'Certainly dear. There's no one in the bunker,' replied her husband.

'What do you think of Percy being elected captain of the club?' questioned Harry.
'He's the best captain drinks can buy,' answered Ian.

If looks could kill, a lot of people would die with a golf club in their hands.

'I hear you've given up playing golf,' said Mark.
'I had to give it up for health reasons,' sighed Bob.
'But I thought the doctor told you to play golf for your health,' countered Mark.
'He did,' answered Mark ruefully. 'But my wife told me she'd kill me if I played again!'

'As a new member, how do you like the greens?' enquired the club secretary.
'Charming couple,' replied the new member, 'charming.'

It was a poor shot and landed in a bunker. The player took two blasts which almost formed a sandstorm but did not move the ball.

'A couple more shots like that,' shouted his cheerful opponent, 'and you may strike oil.'

The two golfers had quite a number of drinks before they set off from the clubhouse to play eighteen holes.

As they unsteadily approached a green one player asked, 'What green is this?'

'Dunno,' replied the other player. 'I don't live around here.'

The funny thing about golf is that bankers who deal in millions can't count six strokes from tee to green.

An angry wife greeted her husband when he returned from playing golf. 'Well, who is she?'

'Who is who?' asked her husband.

'Don't play innocent with me. Who is she?' demanded his wife.

'I don't know what you mean,' protested the husband.

'You know very well what I mean,' stormed the wife. 'Who is the other woman?'

'There is no other woman,' cried her husband.

'Well, only half an hour ago I heard two women talking in the supermarket and one said she had just come from the golf club and had seen you get a birdie on the seventh green.'

'How does one meet new people at this club?' the recently enrolled member asked the club secretary.

'Try picking up the wrong golf ball,' the secretary replied dryly.

'How can I cut down on my strokes?' asked the golfer when he cornered the professional in the shop.

'Why not take up cricket?' said the ever helpful professional.

Colonel Windsor had reached the seventh green and was bending down to mark his ball when he was struck very hard on the backside by a golf ball. He picked up the offending object and walked to the lady who had played it.

'Madam,' he rumbled, thrusting the ball at her, 'the hole at which you should have been aiming has a flag in it!'

The bishop and the bank manager were playing their weekly game of golf and the bishop was having a terrible time. He hooked, he sliced, he never cleared a sand trap or water hazard, and the shortest of putts eluded him. His face was almost purple and his breathing heavy when he used language even the bank manager hadn't heard.

'I'll have to give it up! I'll have to give it up!' shouted the bishop.

'What?' cried his horrified companion. 'Give up golf?'

'No, you noodle-nut!' yelled the bishop. 'Give up the church!'

At the annual golf club dinner one should never forget to toast a faithful caddie – just one of those little things that count.

'Is Clark a good golfer?'
   'Well, let me put it this way, he doesn't use a scorecard, he carries a calculator.'

The four men who played a game of golf every Sunday morning were discussing the problem of getting away from their wives to play.
   'No problem,' said the first golfer. 'I just tell her I'm going to play golf and that's all there is about it. If she doesn't like it – tough!'
   'I make sure she has a couple of really stiff drinks on a Saturday night and she just snoozes away on a Sunday morning,' contributed the second golfer.
   'Our family doctor is a friend of mine, so I said he had recommended it,' confided the third golfer. 'He'll back me up.'
   'Well,' said the fourth golfer, 'I set the alarm for six-thirty, I nudge my wife and asked her if it's going to be golf course or intercourse, and I haven't missed a Sunday yet!'

The vicar called at the home of Mr and Mrs Smith and was greeted by Mrs Smith who invited him in for a cup of tea which he accepted.
   'I really wanted to have a word with your husband because I have heard that James is in the habit of going to the golf club on

a Sunday morning instead of attending church,' rebuked the vicar as he sipped his tea.

'Ah, but he doesn't play golf,' said Mrs Smith helpfully. 'He only goes down for a couple of drinks and a game of snooker.'

'Coming out for a drink, Peter?' asked Gerry.

'Not today, O'Rourke is playing in the Ulster Open,' answered Peter.

'Well, what about next weekend?'

'Can't make it. O'Rourke is playing in the Irish Open.'

'Next week?'

'No, O'Rourke is playing in the British Open.'

'Why the change of game? Your game was always cricket but now you spend your time watching O'Rourke playing golf,' pointed out Gerry.

'I don't watch O'Rourke playing golf,' replied Peter, 'but whenever he plays I sleep with his wife.'

'If I were you I'd take up golf for my health,' said the doctor after examining a patient.

'But doctor, I do play golf,' replied the man.

'In that case, I'd stop.'

A golfer, a witness in an accident case, described himself as the best amateur golfer in the United Kingdom.

'Modest, aren't you?' commented the barrister.

'Ordinarily yes, but I am now under oath,' replied the golfer.

Tony was playing golf in the west of Ireland when he saw a very large dog trotting down the fairway carrying what appeared to be a green doll. Tony then saw it was not a doll but was in fact a leprechaun, so he threatened the dog with his club and the dog dropped the leprechaun and ran away.

'Thank you,' said the leprechaun, standing up and brushing himself down. 'You are very kind, that dog really had me.'

'Could you not have used your magic powers to get free?' asked Tony.

'I only have magic powers when I'm wearing my green hat,' said the little green figure, 'and the dog knocked it off.'

The leprechaun retrieved his hat and said to Tony, 'For your help and kindness I must reward you. So please take this.'

'What is it?' asked Tony.

'It is a magic golf ball and will do as you command. If you say "Magic ball, the green", it will land on the green. If you say "Magic ball, the cup", it will drop into the cup. Always keep the ball in the box unless you are going to instruct it to do some task.'

As he spoke the leprechaun handed Tony a green box and then he disappeared in a green mist.

On his return home Tony dashed into the locker room at his club and gleefully shouted to his friends, 'Look, I have a magic golf ball. All I do is take it out of the box and say "Magic ball, the green", and it will land on the green. Or if I want it to drop into the hole it will.'

'A lot of nonsense,' retorted Denis snatching the box and taking out the ball. 'Magic ball my arse – ooooOO!'

'Hello, Dr Ford speaking,' said the doctor, lifting the telephone.

'Hello, Dick, Len Fowler here,' said the voice.

'Yes, Len.'

'Dick, I was in the back garden trying to improve my swing by using a plastic ball and the baby got to my bag and swallowed all my tees.'

'My God!' exclaimed the doctor. 'I'll be over immediately. What are you doing in the meantime?'

'Oh, I thought I'd do a spot of putting.'

The patient was not happy about the suggestion of an operation and was seeking comfort and assurance. 'After this operation, doctor, will I be able to play golf?'

'You most certainly will,' replied the doctor with a tone of confidence.

'That's wonderful,' said the patient. 'I could never play it before.'

The husband returned home from work and read the note from his wife informing him she had gone to play golf. He was in the shower when she came home and he shouted, 'Hello, darling, how was the golf?'

'Wonderful, dear, wonderful,' answered his wife.

'Good. What did you go round in?'

'My cream sweater and the peach cords I bought when we were on holiday.'

The golf club captain was charged with trying to kill a very troublesome woman member during a mixed foursome.

The entire membership of the club pleaded with the judge to give him another chance.

'I've just hit a hole in one!' shouted the golfer, dancing with joy.

'Oh, isn't that nice,' remarked his wife. 'Do it again dear, I didn't see it.'

'Whatever are you doing?' exclaimed the surprised wife when she walked into the bedroom to find her husband standing naked in front of a full-length mirror swinging a golf club.

'Well,' said her husband, 'the club professional told me I wasn't improving and I was to practise ball control so I thought I'd have a look to see what was going wrong.'

'The professional at the club says I play golf like Norman,' boasted the husband.

'Really,' said his wife, 'Greg or Barry?'

'Golly!' exclaimed Kevin. 'What a club this is. I've never seen such a group of golfers. All have broad shoulders, big hands, thick thighs . . .'

'Yes,' cut in Rory, a club member, 'and the men are the same.'

It was Paddy's first game of golf and when he came to drive off he placed the ball on the ground.

'What about your tee?' asked Michael.

'I'm not hungry. We'll play golf first,' replied Paddy.

Notice on the wall of a locker room in a golf club in Northern Ireland:

If a ball comes to rest in dangerous proximity to an unexploded bomb or land mine, the player may drop another ball at a safe distance, providing it is no nearer the hole, without penalty.

Tom dashed into the locker room and holding up a golf ball cried, 'Look at this!'

'Looks like a golf ball to me,' observed Ken.

'Yes, but it's not just an ordinary golf ball,' gushed Tom. 'This is an unloseable golf ball, it cannot be lost.'

'What do you mean, can't be lost, any ball can be lost,' argued Ken.

'Not this one. When you hit it into the rough, the woods or water it sends out a signal so you can locate it,' insisted Tom.

'Where did you get it?'

'I made a swap with Paul. I gave him six Golden Specials balls for it,' said Tom.

'Where did Paul get it?' asked Ken.

'He found it!'

'The sporting aspect has gone right out of golf,' complained Reggie as he stalked into the locker room.

'What makes you say that?' asked a fellow golfer.

'My opponent wouldn't even concede a two-foot putt,' explained Reggie.

'So what?'

'So it cost me a stroke, that's what!'

There are two kinds of people. Those who play golf and those who don't.

Trouble is, they are usually married to each other.

Barry was mad about golf and never tired of talking about it. His putting, his chip shots, the sand traps, the greens, the caddies and his hole in one.

All this golf talk was driving his wife crazy and one day she howled, 'For Christ's sake talk about something other than golf. I'm fed up listening about golf! Golf! Golf! Golf!'

'Well what do you want to talk about?' asked Barry.

'Anything at all as long as it isn't golf. Talk about sex for a change,' cried his wife.

'Fair enough,' replied Barry. 'I wonder who my caddie is screwing these days?'

The club professional had just returned from a three-day tournament and was called to the secretary's office to explain his poor display to the captain and the chairman.

'That was a very poor show, John,' admonished the chairman glancing at the scoresheet. 'Your figures for the three rounds were 69, 88 and 69, that's a very poor show indeed and you've let the club down.'

'Sorry about that,' apologized the professional.

'What happened on the second day when you took 88?' asked the chairman.

'That's the day my wife was having her baby and I was very nervous,' explained the professional.

'Really John, that's not good enough,' reprimanded the chairman. 'If you're going to play for this club you'll have to get your priorities right!'

'What do you think about this mixed foursome, do you think we should accept the invitation to play?' queried Ruth.

'I don't really care,' answered Agnes. 'I'll abide by your decision.'

'Well, I don't really care for mixed foursomes,' commented Ruth. 'All the men talk about is golf.'

Alan would never concede a stroke. He had been known to play from the most impossible positions, so one day when he hooked a ball which landed on the lap of a woman sitting on the bank, his companions watched with interest.

Alan viewed the situation, selected a wedge from his bag and said, 'Brace yourself dear, this may smart a little.'

All is fair in love and golf.

Angus McTavis was playing golf one very cold day on a coastal course in the north of Scotland. At the end of the round he slipped something into the caddie's hand and said kindly, 'That's for a glass of hot whisky, laddie.'

The caddie opened his hand to find a lump of sugar.

The manager of a sports shop was rather surprised when the 'madam' of a local house of pleasure came in and asked to see some golf balls.

'This is the best ball we have,' said the manager. 'If you purchase this brand of ball we print your name on it free of charge.'

'Wonderful,' said the lady. 'If you print my telephone number on it as well I'll take twelve dozen.'

'Frankly, Eric, I don't understand you,' muttered Barry. 'First you slice your ball into the rough, then into the woods, then you hook it out of bounds, after that you nearly decapitate old Charlie Woodlee with it, then you drive it into the water and you still insist on finding it.'

'I have to find it,' replied Eric. 'It's my lucky ball.'

The elderly man stood gazing out of the clubhouse window and said in a sad tone, 'Golf is such a cruel game.'

'Cruel?' queried his companion. 'Why do you say cruel?'

'Well,' replied the elderly golfer, 'now that I'm wealthy enough to afford lost balls, I can't hit them far enough to lose them.'

Rosemary Murray had just been presented with the cup for being the best lady player in the club and was being interviewed by a reporter from the local paper. When he asked her age Rosemary stalled for a moment then murmured softly, 'Well, you might say I'm approaching forty.' Seeing some raised eyebrows among her companions she continued, 'Perhaps not so much an approach as a putt.'

'And a very short putt at that,' loudly whispered one of the women.

'More like a hole in one,' commented another woman.

Angus McDonald, who had played golf for many years on a course near Fife, arrived home one day and told his wife he was giving up the game.

His wife was shocked, for she knew how much he loved golf, so she asked, 'Why are you giving up golf?'

'I lost ma ball,' replied Angus.

Frank was a confirmed bachelor so he surprised the other members of the club when he announced he was getting married in two weeks. He bought drinks for those present and after the congratulations and giggles of glee had died down he cornered the club professional.

'Do you remember, Tom,' said Frank, 'you told me that my whippy shaft would get me into trouble?'

'Indeed I do,' replied the professional.

'Oh, Christ, Tom,' moaned Frank. 'Did it get me into trouble!'

The lady was of ample proportions and, after much grunting and wriggling, belted the ball with unbridled hatred. She succeeded in digging out a deep and extensive divot which travelled farther than the ball.

She went and poked the large piece of sod with her club. 'What should I do with this?' she asked the caddie.

'The rules state you must replace it in the hole you just dug it out of,' answered the caddie. 'However, in your case I'd take it home and practise on it.'

'Robert is a golfer with great spirit,' observed Jack. 'He lost ten games in a row.'

'I bet he was discouraged,' remarked Jim.

'Not a bit of it,' said Jack. 'He went out and lost ten more.'

The rather heavily built woman was doing her best to hack her way round the course. After playing the first hole she panted to the caddie, 'How many strokes?'

'I've no idea,' replied the caddie.

'You're a caddie and you don't know how many strokes?' grumbled the woman.

'Missus, it's not a caddie you need, it's an accountant!'

'Where's your husband?' asked Freda.

'On the golf course,' replied Joan.

'Is he playing in a big match?'

'No, he's playing with himself.'

'Oh? I thought only small boys did that.'

The girl interviewer, in her sexiest voice, asked the handsome world-famous golfer, 'What is your favourite course?' 'Inter,' replied the smiling golfer.

The golfer walked into the professional's shop and said, 'George, what can I do to lower my handicap? Surely you must have something in the shop to help me.'

'Certainly, Ben, no problem. Here you are,' offered George.

'But, George,' protested Ben, 'this is just a pencil.'

'Yes, but it has an eraser attached.'

The two women had just been introduced and were standing talking and the conversation came round to golf. 'Oh, I'm a golf widow,' said one, 'my husband spends more time on the golf course than he spends at home.'

'I'm also a golf widow,' said the other woman.

'Does your husband spend his time on the golf course too?' questioned the first woman.

'No, he was killed when he fell out of a tree trying to play a stroke rather than concede it!' answered the woman with a sad shake of her head.

A famous golfer died and went to the great clubhouse in the sky where he was greeted by a saint and asked if he had anything to confess before passing through the gates.

'Well, there is one thing,' confessed the golfer. 'I was playing for Ireland against England and my opponent and I both played into the rough. I found the balls which were lying together and

I kicked his ball into an unplayable position. That action probably won the match for us but it has worried me ever since.'

'Think nothing of it, my son, not a thing to worry about, forget it ever happened,' said the saint with a smile.

'Oh, that's wonderful,' cried the golfer. 'Thank you very much St Peter.'

'Oh, by the way, I'm not St Peter,' said the saint cheerily, 'I'm St Patrick.'

M iss Starlet arrived for her first golf lesson dressed more for a fashion show than golf.

'Do you have clubs?' asked the professional.

'Of course I have clubs,' Miss Starlet replied.

'What's your driver like?'

'Oh, he's very sweet, tall and rather good-looking. He is wearing a blue uniform and standing beside my Rolls Royce.'

F or Sale: Set of golf clubs at bargain price of £100. Telephone 242424 before six o'clock. If a man answers, hang up.

T he two golfers were supporting the bar at the nineteenth and one said, 'I hear you're not playing for the club team against Moreton next Saturday.'

'I should say not,' replied the other golfer, draining his glass. 'Not after what the captain said to me on Sunday.'

'Oh?' asked the other golfer, signalling for two more drinks, 'What did he say?'

'You're dropped!'

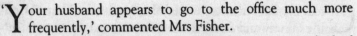

'Your husband appears to go to the office much more frequently,' commented Mrs Fisher.

'Yes,' said Mrs Reid, 'his doctor said it was important he had something to take his mind off golf.'

It is generally known that Lady Thatcher does not share her husband's love of golf. One night at a reception she asked a man why he had become a professional golfer.

'Probably because my father was a professional golfer,' replied the golfer.

'What would have happened if he had been a criminal?' came the icy question.

'Well, in that case,' the golfer answered, 'I would have become a politician.'

'How can I prevent topping the ball when I hit it?' asked O'Toole.

'Try turning it upside down,' suggested O'Flynn.

A man on holiday was playing golf with a club member and they were all square at the seventh.

'How long have you been playing golf?' enquired the club member.

'Oh, about four months,' was the reply.

'Well, you certainly play a very good game,' complimented the club member.'

'I ought to,' sighed the visitor. 'It took me seven years to learn.'

Greer played well until the eighth when he hooked a ball off the fairway and almost hit a man. He ran over to the man and said, 'Sorry about that.'

'Why the hell didn't you yell "Fore"?' shouted the man.

'I hadn't time to shout,' protested Greer.

'You had time enough to shout "Oh, bollocks",' countered the man.

Terry and William were on holiday in Spain and Terry suggested a game of golf.

'What?' said William. 'In this heat? Only a fool would play golf today.'

'Great,' replied Terry, 'we shouldn't have any trouble getting a game.'

George had been putting for two hours in his back garden when the telephone rang. Carefully he put down his putter and lifted the telephone. 'Hello?'

'Hello, George,' came the voice, 'Roger here, rang to see if you care for a game on Saturday.'

'Fine old chap, nine o'clock on the tee,' answered George. 'But you'll beat me easily – I haven't touched a club for weeks . . .'

Lost your job as a caddie?' asked the father.

'Yes,' replied his son. 'I could do the job all right, but I couldn't learn not to laugh.'

'Darling,' cried the husband as he entered the house, 'I have just bought a present for the person I love most in all the world.'

'And what are your new golf clubs like?' asked his wife in an icy tone.

Gerry entered the locker room and stripped off to have a shower. He removed his shirt to reveal he was wearing a brassiere.

'When did you start wearing that thing?' asked an interested Jack.

'Since my wife found it in the back seat of my car,' replied Gerry.

'I see your wife has taken up golf,' remarked Joe.

'Yes, indeed,' nodded James.

'How is she doing?'

'Well, she's the only golfer I know who complains she has an unplayable lie when she places the ball on the tee,' sighed James.

David stalked into the locker room, threw his clubs on the floor, sat on the bench and muttered, 'Bloody hell! Bloody hell!'

'I just don't know how you managed to take seventeen for that hole. It's an easy par four, no sand traps, no water, easy,' went on Bert. 'So how the hell did you take seventeen?'

'Easy,' hissed David. 'I missed a short putt for sixteen!'

A gospel preacher from a southern state in the USA was on a visit to London and was playing golf with an English friend. At the seventh hole he missed a very short putt but did not say a word.

'I must say that's very commendable of you,' said the Englishman. 'If I had missed a putt like that my language would have turned the air blue.'

'Can't use bad language,' drawled the preacher. 'But let me tell you, after a shot like that I spit and where I spit the grass never grows again!'

'You're a hopeless, no good lay-about,' the father shouted at his son. 'Are you going to spend the rest of your life tramping around a golf course?'

'No, dad,' replied the son. 'I was hoping you would buy me a buggy.'

B ishop Flynn and Father Casey prepared to tee off. Both men were good players and Father Casey was intent on beating his bishop as this was the first time they had played in opposition.

They were all square at the sixth and Father Casey had a short putt to give him a birdie and take the lead. He viewed the situation with great care and putted. The ball rimmed the hole but did not drop. Both men stared at it in silence.

'Father Casey, enough of that!' said the bishop sharply. 'That's the most obscene silence I've ever heard!'

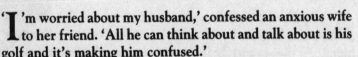

'**I**'m worried about my husband,' confessed an anxious wife to her friend. 'All he can think about and talk about is his golf and it's making him confused.'

'Why, what has he done?' enquired her friend.

'Well, he's worried about his tee shots so he went down to the school of motoring and enrolled for an advanced driving course!' cried the wife.

'**C**addie,' shouted the golfer,' isn't Major Saunders out of that bunker yet?'

'Not yet,' replied the caddie.

'How many strokes has he had?' asked the golfer.

'Seventeen ordinary and one apoplectic!'

A keen golfer had a charming girl sitting on his right at dinner and gave her graphic descriptions of his achievements on the course, giving her little time to say more than 'Oh, really?'

As they sipped brandy the golfer said, 'I've been doing all the talking, I hope I haven't bored you with my golf stories.'

'There's just one thing,' said the girl.

'What's that?' asked the golfer.

'What *is* golf?'

'**W**hat do you think would go well with my purple and peach golf socks?' asked the wife.

'Hip boots,' replied her husband.

The two Irishmen were strolling along the fairway when they heard the warning shout 'Fore!' and a golf ball whizzed past them. Immediately the two men threw themselves to the ground and one gasped, 'Don't move! There must be three more to come!'

The husband took his wife out for her first game of golf and, placing the ball on a tee, said, 'Do you see that flag?'

'Yes,' said his wife, peering ahead.

'Well, aim the ball at that,' instructed her husband.

The lady took a big swing at the ball which sailed gracefully through the air, landed on the green, rolled forward and dropped into the cup.

'Oh, dear,' cried the wife, 'now I've lost my ball!'

Reggie Prescott-Lloyd was sitting in the clubhouse bar sipping a brandy when he was joined by his friend Ronald Bellingham-Spencer.

'Reggie, I must speak to you,' said Ronald.

'Do sit down old boy and have a drink,' invited Reggie, waving for another drink.

'Reggie, what I'm going to say is very painful but it must be said. I love your wife and want to marry her,' stated Ronald firmly.

'But she is married – to me,' pointed out Reggie.

'Yes, but divorce would take care of that.'

'Divorce indeed! Such a messy business. The dogs and horses have to be considered. Lots of bother you know. Why are you telling me? Why didn't Margaret tell me about this affair?'

queried Reggie.

'Well, she thought you might be upset and want to challenge me to a duel,' confessed Ronald.

'Good gad! Do they still do that sort of thing? I don't mind getting up at dawn for a game of golf but I'm damned if I'm going to get up that early for a duel,' snorted Reggie.

'Well, let's play golf for her,' proposed Ronald. 'The winner to take the lady.'

'That's a jolly good idea,' agreed Reggie. 'And to make the game interesting let's have a £10 bet on it.'

'Your husband appears to be playing much better since he adopted a new stance,' pointed out Elizabeth.

'Same stance,' said Ruth. 'New husband.'